Stay Healthy!

Why Do We Need to Eat?

Angela Royston

Heinemann Library
Chicago, Illinois

© 2006 Heinemann Library
a division of Reed Elsevier Inc.
Chicago, Illinois

Customer Service   888–454–2279

Visit our website at www.heinemannlibrary.com

Photo research by Ruth Blair, Ginny Stroud-Lewis
Designed by Jo Hinton-Malivoire, bigtop
Printed and bound in China by South China Printing Company

10 09 08 07 06
10 9 8 7 6 5 4 3 2 1

Library of Congress Cataloging-in-Publication Data
Royston, Angela.
 Why do we need to eat? / Angela Royston.
     p. cm. -- (Stay healthy!)
 Includes bibliographical references and index.
 ISBN 1-4034-7606-3 (library binding-hardcover) -- ISBN 1-4034-7611-X
(pbk.) 1. Nutrition--Juvenile literature. I. Title. II. Series.
 RA784.R6983 2006
 613.2--dc22

                                              2005010376

Acknowledgments
The author and publisher are grateful to the following for permission to reproduce copyright material:
Alamy p.7 top, 10, 12, 15(Loetscher Chlaus), 16(Jim West), 23a; Corbis pp.5, 19, 23e; Getty Images pp7(bottom), 8(The Image Bank), p.9(Photodisc), p.21 (Taxi); Harcourt Education pp.4, 12, 23c (Gareth Boden), pp.6, 11, 13, 14, 17, 18, 20, 22, 23b-d(Tudor Photography).

Cover photograph of boys eating watermelons reproduced with permission of Corbis. Back cover images reproduced with permission of Harcourt Education/Gareth Boden and Tudor Photography.

Every effort has been made to contact copyright holders of any material reproduced in this book. Any omissions will be rectified in subsequent printings if notice is given to the publisher.

The author and publisher would like to thank Dr. Sarah Schencker, Dietitian, for her comments in the preparation of this book.

Some words are shown in bold, **like this.** You can find them in the picture glossary on page 23.

Contents

Why Do You Need to Eat?

You need to eat because food gives you **energy** and **nutrients**.

Your body needs these to work properly.

You should eat lots of different kinds of food.

What Do You Need to Eat the Most Of?

pasta

bread

potato

rice

Your body needs lots of food such as rice and pasta.

This is **starchy** food. Starchy food gives you **energy**.

Everything you do uses energy.

Who do you think is using the most energy here?

The children pushing scooters and riding bikes use the most **energy**.

The girl reading does not use as much energy.

You use energy even when you sleep!

What Food Helps You Grow?

Food that has **protein** in it helps you to grow.

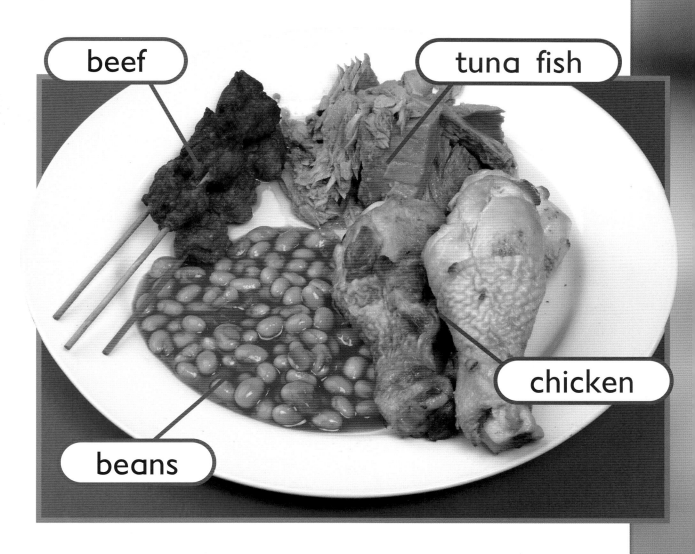

beef

tuna fish

chicken

beans

All of these foods have protein in them.

Which of them is not meat or fish?

veggie burger

tofu

Beans are not meat but have **protein** in them.

Tofu and veggie burgers are made from a kind of bean.

cheese

Children need lots of protein because they are still growing.

Cheese has protein in it, too.

Why Do You Need Food to Keep Warm?

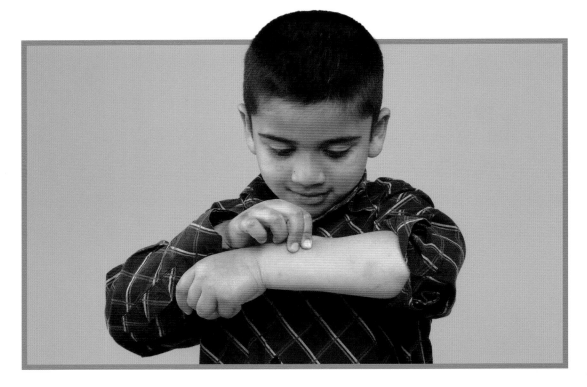

Your body stores extra **energy** from your food.

Some of this energy is stored as fat.

There is a layer of fat under
your skin.

It helps to keep you warm.

Why Do You Need to Eat Fruit and Vegetables?

Fruit and vegetables have lots of fiber.

Fiber helps your body to get rid of waste.

bread

broccoli

cereal

nuts

celery

orange

These foods have fiber.

Which of them are vegetables?

Celery and broccoli are vegetables.

Fruit and vegetables have **vitamins** and **minerals** in them.

Your body needs different vitamins
and minerals to work properly.

What Food Makes Your Bones Strong?

Food that has calcium makes your bones strong.

Does milk have calcium?

Milk, cheese, and yogurt all have calcium.

Calcium makes your teeth strong, too.

Make Some Healthy Coleslaw!

1. Wash some cabbage, a carrot, and an apple.

2. Peel the carrot.

3. Grate the cabbage, carrot, and apple.

4. Mix these in a bowl with some natural yogurt.

5. Enjoy eating your healthy coleslaw!

Glossary

 **energy** power you need to move or do anything

 **mineral** kind of chemical that is in some foods that your body needs to be healthy

 **nutrient** chemical that is in food that your body needs to be healthy

 **protein** kind of food that helps you grow

 **starchy** type of food that gives you energy

 **vitamin** nutrient made by plants and animals

Index

Note to Parents and Teachers

Reading nonfiction texts for information is an important part of a child's literacy development. Readers can be encouraged to ask simple questions and then use the text to find the answers. Most chapters in this book begin with a question. Read the questions together. Look at the pictures. Talk about what the answer might be. Then read the text to find out if your predictions were correct. To develop readers' inquiry skills, encourage them to think of other questions they might ask about the topic. Discuss where you could find the answers. Assist children in using the contents page, picture glossary, and index to practice research skills and new vocabulary.